TRUSTING

GOD

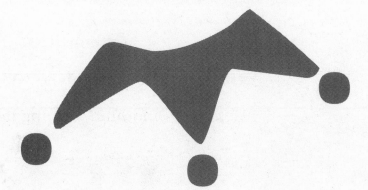

TRUSTING GOD

Carine Mackenzie

CF4•K

© Copyright 2007 Carine Mackenzie
ISBN 978-1-84550-271-3
Published in 2007 by
Christian Focus Publications,
Geanies House, Fearn, Tain
Ross-shire, IV20 1TW,
Great Britain
Cover design by Daniel van Straaten
Cover illustration by Jeff Anderson
Printed and bound by Nørhaven Paperback A/S

The Scripture version used throughout this book is The King James, Authorised version.

PSALM 20:6-8

Now know I that the LORD saveth his anointed;

he will hear him from his holy heaven

with the saving strength of his right hand.

Some trust in chariots, and some in horses:

but we will remember the name of

the LORD our God.

They are brought down and fallen:

but we are risen, and stand upright.

Contents

1. A Strong Tower:

Introducing the Name of God 9

2. I am who I am:

God Introduces Himself 11

3. Jehovah Jireh:

The Lord Will Provide 15

4. Jehovah Nissi:

The Lord Is My Banner 23

5. Jehovah Rohi:

The Lord is my Shepherd 31

6. Jehovah Rophi:

The Lord Who Heals 39

7. Jehovah Shalom:

The Lord is Peace 47

8. Jehovah Shammah:

The Lord is There 57

9. Jehovah Tsidkenu:

The Lord our Righteousness 65

10. Jehovah Maccaddeshem:

The LORD who sanctifies...........................77

11. Jehovah Sabaoth:

LORD of Hosts. 83

1. A STRONG TOWER

INTRODUCING THE NAME OF GOD

The name of God is very important. One of the commandments given by God tells us that we must not take the name of the Lord in vain. We must not use it carelessly or without realising how great God is.

The Bible tells us that God's name is great, glorious, everlasting, exalted, holy and wonderful.

"The name of the Lord is a strong tower; the righteous run into it and are safe," says one of the Proverbs. God's name displays his power and mercy and wisdom which his people can safely trust in.

God's name is to be exalted. David the psalmist said, "O magnify the Lord with me. Let us exalt his name together" Psalm 34:3.

"I will praise thy name, O Lord, for it is good" Psalm 54:6.

God's people love his name.

2. I AM WHO I AM

GOD INTRODUCES HIMSELF

While Moses was looking after his father in law's sheep in the desert he saw what must have been an amazing sight. A bush was ablaze but the fire did not consume it. God spoke from the bush.

"Take off your shoes for you are standing on holy ground."

God explained to Moses that he was to lead his people out of slavery in Egypt to the Promised Land of Canaan. Moses did not feel equal to the task but God assured him that he would be with him.

"If I tell the people of Israel that the God of their fathers has sent me to lead them," said Moses to God, "they will say 'What is His name?' What shall I say to them?"

God replied, "I AM WHO I AM. Tell them I AM has sent me to you."

This name shows that God has always existed, that He is now and that He always will exist. This is the name which is written as Yahweh in Hebrew. In our Bibles this is translated as the LORD with capital letters.

3. JEHOVAH JIREH

THE LORD WILL PROVIDE

Each year a list is compiled of the most

popular names given to babies born in the

year. The list changes slightly year on year.

One year Jack and Emma might be top, the

next David and Amy. If the name is top of the list it means that many children have been given that name during the year.

Some people give their baby a much more individual name – something very unusual that they think no one else would have. But even the most unusual name can be copied.

God has many names that are truly unique. No one else is worthy of these names. One of these names is Jehovah Jireh – meaning the Lord will provide.

Abraham and Sarah were given a son when they were both very old. God had made a promise to Abraham that he would be the father of many nations, even of kings.

Sarah would be blessed as the mother of many nations. You can read about this in Genesis 17:16.

At last when Abraham was 100 years old and Sarah 90, their son Isaac was born.

One day when Isaac was older, God put Abraham's faith to the test.

God told Abraham "Take your son Isaac and go to Mount Moriah. Offer up your son as a sacrifice there."

Abraham obeyed.

But what would happen to God's promise if Isaac was killed? Abraham believed in God. His promise is true.

Abraham and Isaac went together up the mountain. Isaac carried the wood for the sacrificial fire and Abraham took the fire and the knife. Isaac was puzzled. "Father," he asked, "where is the lamb for the burnt offering?"

"My son, God will provide a lamb for the offering," Abraham replied.

Abraham built an altar and laid the wood on it, tied Isaac his son to the wood and took the knife in his hand.

Just then the angel of the Lord called out and stopped him. "Don't touch your son. Now I know that you fear God, seeing you did not keep your only son from me."

Abraham then noticed in a bush a ram caught by its horns. This was God provision.

Abraham called the place Jehovah Jireh – The Lord will Provide.

The Lord is Jehovah Jireh for us too. He has made the great provision of a sacrifice for our sin, the Lord Jesus Christ. When John the Baptist saw Jesus, he said "Behold the Lamb of God who takes away the sin of the world" John 1:29. God did indeed provide a lamb for the sacrifice. Jesus went to Calvary carrying the wood as Isaac did. His Father did not spare him, but delivered him up for his people - those whom the

Father draws to himself and whom he will never cast away.

Jehovah Jireh has provided many wonderful things for his people, but the most amazing is the Saviour, Jesus Christ.

 Think Spot: Think about the things that God provides for you every day.

 Thank Spot: Have you ever thanked God for Jesus? He is the best gift you could ever have.

BIBLE SEARCH

Look up the verses to find some gifts that God has provided for his people.

1. "For God so loved the world, that he gave his only begotten Son, that whosoever believeth in him should not perish, but have _____ _____" John 3:16.

2. "Him hath God exalted with his right hand to be a Prince and a Saviour, for to give _____to Israel and _____ __ ____"Acts 5:31.

3. "He hath clothed me with the garments of _____, he hath covered me with the robe of _____ " Isaiah 61:10.

4. "Think soberly according as God hath dealt to every man the measure of _____" Romans 12:3.

5. "Who shall separate us from the _____ of Christ?" Romans 8:35.

6. "The _____ of God, which passeth all understanding, shall keep your hearts and minds through Christ Jesus" Philippians 4:7.

7. "The ____ of the Lord is your strength" Nehemiah 8:10.

8. "The Lord gave the _____: great was the company of those that published it" Psalm 68:11.

9. "Trust in the living God who giveth us _____ ____ _____ to enjoy" 1 Timothy 6:17.

4. JEHOVAH NISSI

THE LORD IS MY BANNER

Have you ever watched the Trooping of

the Colour ceremony on the television?

Hundreds of splendid guardsmen march

on Horse Guard's Parade in London before

the Queen. A special flag or banner known as the Colour is displayed to the assembled soldiers. This impressive ceremony is a tradition. It first began many years ago when the rallying flag would be shown to the soldiers before they went into battle. The soldiers would then recognise their army banner and know where to turn to in times of danger and confusion.

The people of Amalek fought the children of Israel on their journey to the Promised Land. Joshua was the chosen army general who led the troops of Israel.

"I will stand on the top of the hill," said Moses, "with the rod of God in my hand."

Moses, Aaron and Hur went up to the top of the hill and watched the battle below.

When Moses held up his hand, appealing to God in prayer, Joshua and his soldiers were victorious. But when his hand fell down then the enemy, Amalek, won. If you have ever tried holding up your hands for a long time, you will know how hard it is.

Moses sat down on a big stone. Aaron and Hur supported his hands, one on each side. By the end of the day, Joshua and the Israelite army had a great victory, through the help and power of the great God.

After the victory Moses built an altar to God and called its name Jehovah Nissi, "The

Lord is My Banner". God was the rallying point, the place of safety and direction.

The Lord's people are in a battle today too, a battle against sin and the evil one. Our banner or rallying point is the Lord Jehovah. We must take our direction from him and rely on his resources so that we will be victorious in the end. Jesus Christ is the rallying point "evidently set forth, crucified among you," Galatians 3:1. He is gathering his people together to himself.

David describes God and his truth as a rallying point for his troubled people. "You have given a banner to those who fear you that it may be displayed because of the truth," Psalm 60:4.

We cannot fight alone or in our own strength. We need to be always looking for Jesus, trusting in him and his power and might. His word of truth is a sure rallying point for us in the battle against sin.

Just as Moses kept his hands up towards heaven, interceding for victory for his people. We too should be watching and praying, asking Jehovah Nissi for the victory.

 Think Spot: What does your national flag look like? How is Jesus like a banner or flag?

 Thank Spot: Thank God that you can always come to him with your troubles.

BIBLE SEARCH

The initials of the missing words spell
out something in the story.

1. "Behold I will lift up mine hand to the
Gentiles and set up _____ standard to the
people" Isaiah 49:22.

2. "Now we beseech _____ brethren, by the
coming of our Lord Jesus Christ and by our
gathering together unto him"
 2 Thessalonians 2:1.

3. "He brought me to the _____
house, and his banner over me was love"
Song of Solomon 2:4.

4. "O foolish Galatians, who hath bewitched

you, that ye should not obey the truth, before whose eyes Jesus Christ hath been evidently set forth, crucified _____ you?" Galatians 3:1.

5. "And he will lift up an ensign to the _____ from far" Isaiah 5:26.

6. "The _____ of the Lord is a strong tower: The righteous runneth into it and is safe" Proverbs 18:10.

7. "And in that day there shall be a root of Jesse, which shall stand for an _____ of the people" Isaiah 11:10.

8. "We will _____ in thy salvation" Psalm 20:5.

Answer: _____   _____

5. JEHOVAH ROHI

THE LORD IS MY SHEPHERD

God has given us his word, so that we can learn about him. He has used many different words to explain what he is like and what he does.

God tells us that he is Jehovah Rohi – the Lord my Shepherd.

The shepherd feeds the sheep, bringing them to pasture and water. God feeds his people. Our daily food comes from God and we should thank him for his goodness to us.

He also feeds us with food for the soul. "For he satisfieth the longing soul, and filleth the hungry soul with goodness" Psalm 107:9. The Lord Jesus Christ is the only one that will truly satisfy our souls.

A godly man once said, "Nothing less than Christ will satisfy, and when you find him, nothing more could be desired." May we pray that we would find this true satisfaction from Jehovah Rohi – our Shepherd.

The shepherd in eastern countries leads his sheep from the front, rather than driving them from behind. He walks in front and the sheep follow him.

Jehovah Rohi, our Shepherd, is a leader to his people. Jesus described himself as the Good Shepherd. "My sheep hear my voice and I know them, and they follow me." Our duty is to listen to his instruction and keep our eyes fixed on him. We should pray that he would lead us by his light and truth, and that he would lead us to himself, our shelter and Saviour.

Sometimes a sheep with a heavy fleece will fall down and roll on to its back. The sheep finds it impossible to roll back on to its feet. The sheep is described as being "cast" or "cast down". The shepherd realises the danger of this and comes to help. If left unattended the sheep would soon die. But a push from the shepherd helps the sheep to its feet again. Once the sheep starts feeding the shepherd knows it will be fine.

Sometimes a follower of Jesus becomes cast down – perhaps by cares or worries, or by falling into sin, or finding it difficult to pray. We then need a push or encouragement from our shepherd. "Why are you cast down, O my soul?" the Psalmist asked himself. The push or encouragement he got was, "Hope thou in God: for I shall yet praise him for the help of his countenance" Psalm 42:5. The word of God is full of encouragements for us to trust in him.

Jehovah Rohi – the Lord our Shepherd – will feed and lead his people. He will tenderly care for and cherish his own dear ones. We should delight in his provision for us in his word and in his Son. We should feed on him and follow him always. Then we are safe for time and eternity.

Think Spot: How often do you feed on food during the day? How often do you think you should feed on God's word?

 Thank Spot: Thank the Lord for providing your soul with the food it needs in God's word. Read it regularly just as you eat food regularly.

BIBLE SEARCH

Find the missing words. The initials of

your answers spell out the story topic.

1. "He restoreth my _____: he leads me

in the paths of righteousness for his name's

sake" Psalm 23:3.

2. "Lead me to the rock that is _____

than I" Psalm 61:2.

3. "O satisfy us _____ with thy mercy;

that we may rejoice and be glad all our

days" Psalm 90:14.

4. "I will abundantly bless her provision:

I will satisfy her _____ with bread"

Psalm 132:15.

5. "*When thou saidst,* Seek ye my face, my

_____ said unto thee, thy face Lord will

I seek" Psalm 27:8.

6. "Who satisfieth thy mouth with good

things; so that thy youth is renewed like the

_____" Psalm 103:5.

7. "Thou art with me; thy _____ and thy

staff they comfort me" Psalm 23:4.

8. "Delight thyself also in the Lord; and he

shall give thee the _____ of thine

heart" Psalm 37:4.

Answer: _____

6. JEHOVAH ROPHI

THE LORD WHO HEALS

I recently burnt my arm on the cooker when I was taking a hot dish out of the oven. The burn was painful for a while and the scar looked very ugly. But eventually the burn healed and the scar is now hardly visible. That simple healing of a burnt arm or a scraped knee is evidence of our loving and powerful God, who made us, provides for our life and who is the source of all healing. We may use an aspirin or antiseptic cream, but the healing is all from God.

One of God's special names is Jehovah Rophi – the LORD who heals.

Moses and the children of Israel crossed the Red Sea miraculously on dry land. God saved them from the Egyptian army chasing them. They walked for three days into the desert. No water was available. They were all so thirsty. When they came to a place called Marah, they thought their problem was solved when they found water. But no, the water there was bitter and undrinkable.

They complained to Moses, "What shall we drink?"

Moses cried out to God for help. God showed him a tree, which Moses took and threw into the water. The water was then made sweet. Their thirst was quenched.

God made a promise at this time to the children of Israel.

"If you will listen to me, and do what is right and obey my commandments, you will not suffer from the diseases which I brought on the Egyptians; for I am the LORD who heals you - Jehovah Rophi."

The Lord Jesus Christ, God the Son, came to this world to suffer and die for his people. One day he was preaching in the synagogue in Nazareth. He read from the book of Isaiah.

"The Spirit of the Lord is upon me," he quoted, "he has anointed me to preach the gospel to the poor, he has sent me to heal the broken-hearted."

Jesus was the fulfilment of that prophecy.

Jesus is the source of all comfort, the one who heals the broken-hearted. He gives healing and restoration to our souls. Our sin and rebellion against God are described as wounds, bruises and putrefying (or rotting) sores. We desperately need healing for our sins. This is provided by the death of Christ. Christ died for the ungodly. "He was wounded for our transgressions, he was bruised for our iniquities: the chastisement of our peace was upon him; and with his stripes we are healed" Isaiah 53:5.

When we are sad, Jehovah Rophi can give us deliverance and healing - causing us to hope in God and give all the praise to him. David said in Psalm 43, that the Lord is "the health of my countenance and my God."

God is the one, the only one, who gives us real hope and encouragement. We may not know what the future brings but we can trust God with the future!

Think Spot: When you feel sad it is a good thing to count how many good things God has given you. This is called counting your blessings. You will soon find you have lots to be thankful for.

 Thank Spot: Once you've counted as many of God's blessings as you can start thanking God for them... start with thanking him for sending his son, Jesus.

BIBLE SEARCH

The initials of the missing words will spell

out something in the story.

1. "Why art thou cast down, O my soul?

And why art thou disquieted within me?

_____ thou in God" Psalm 42:11.

2. "That thy way may be known upon

_____, thy saving health among all

nations" Psalm 67:2.

3. "Lord be merciful unto me: heal my soul;

for I have sinned _____ thee"

Psalm 41:4.

4. "The _____ of the tree were for

the healing of the nations"

Revelations 22:2.

5. "Who forgiveth all thine _____ ;

who healeth all thy diseases" Psalm 103:3.

6. "The people...followed him: and he

received them, and spake unto them of the

kingdom of God and healed them that had

_____ of healing" Luke 9:11.

7. "Is there no balm in _____; is

there no physician there? Why then is not

the health of the daughter of my people

recovered?" Jeremiah 8:22.

Answer: _____

7. JEHOVAH SHALOM

THE LORD IS PEACE

Our world is full of unrest, and war. Every news bulletin tells of bombs, and violence and hatred. Neither soldiers nor politicians can bring peace to these terrible situations.

Even in a family or among colleagues or school mates there is often quarrelling and arguing. This disrupts the harmony of the home or office or playground.

Gideon lived at a time of trouble and war for his nation. The children of Israel had done evil in the sight of the Lord and he had allowed the Midianite enemy to ravage the land for seven years. The land was devastated, the food was stolen but still the nation disobeyed God.

God had a plan for them. He sent an angel to speak to Gideon, who was threshing wheat in a wine press, to hide it from the Midianites.

"The Lord is with thee, thou mighty man of valour," the angel told the frightened Gideon. "Thou shalt save Israel from the hand of the Midianites: have not I sent thee?" said the Lord.

"My family is the weakest in Manasseh and I am the least in my father's house," objected Gideon. He felt very inadequate.

"I will be with you," the Lord promised.

Gideon went to prepare some food as a sacrifice and the Lord graciously waited for him to return.

Following the angel of God's instructions, Gideon put the meat and unleavened cakes on a rock and poured broth over them. The angel reached out a staff and touched the food. Fire sprang up and consumed it. Then the angel vanished from his sight.

Gideon realised that he had been speaking to an angel of the Lord. He was even more afraid.

But God spoke words of comfort to him. "Peace be to you. Do not fear: you shall not die."

Gideon then built an altar to God there. He called it Jehovah Shalom – the Lord is Peace.

Gideon did indeed defeat the Midianites in a wonderful way with God's help. He was given the courage to tear down the altars to the false god Baal, because Jehovah Shalom, the God of Peace was with him even in difficult and dangerous war situations.

Those who love the Lord Jesus Christ, experience God's peace. "Being justified by faith, we have peace with God through our Lord Jesus Christ" Romans 5:1. This peace is not dependant on circumstances. Life may be full of problems and worries and fears, but Jesus has promised his followers his peace. "My peace I give unto you: not as the world giveth, give I unto you. Let not your heart be troubled, neither let it be afraid" John 14:27.

The peace of God surpasses all understanding.

We can trust in the same God of Peace, Jehovah Shalom. His promises are still the same.

 Think Spot: The word of God tells us that God blesses the peacemakers for they shall be called Sons of God. How can you be a peacemaker in your own life?

 Thank Spot: Thank Jesus that he gives you true peace. Ask him for his peace when you feel anxious and worried.

BIBLE SEARCH

The initial letters of the missing words
will spell out something in the story.

1. "These things I have _____ unto you,

that in me ye might have peace" John 16:33.

2. "Let the peace of God rule in your _____,

to the which also ye are called in one body;

and be ye thankful" Colossians 3:15.

3. "For God is not the _____ of

confusion, but of peace" 1 Corinthians 14:33.

4. "Great peace have they which _____ thy

law: and nothing shall offend them" Psalm

119:165.

5. "For he is _____ peace, who hath made both one, and have broken down the middle wall of partition between us" Ephesians 2:14.

6. "For to be carnally _____ is death; but to be spiritually minded is life and peace" Romans 8:6.

7. "And how shall they _____, except they be sent? As it is written, 'How beautiful are the feet of them that preach the gospel of peace, and bring glad tidings of good things!'" Romans 10:15.

8. "Mark the perfect man, and behold the upright: for the _____ of that man is peace" Psalm 37:37.

9. "But the meek shall inherit the earth;

and shall delight themselves in the

_____ of peace" Psalm 37:11.

10. "But he was wounded for our

transgressions, he was bruised for our

iniquities: the _____ of our

peace was upon him; and with his stripes

we are healed" Isaiah 53:5.

11. "Glory to God in the highest, and on

_____ peace, good will toward men" Luke

2:14.

Answer: _____ _____

8. JEHOVAH SHAMMAH

THE LORD IS THERE

Ezekiel was called by God to be a prophet

to his exiled people in Babylon. He used

visions and parables and symbols to

proclaim the message of God. Much of

his message is about condemnation and judgement and punishment for sin. But the promise is given of the coming of the True Shepherd – the Messiah, the Lord Jesus Christ.

The book of Ezekiel ends with "Jehovah Shammah – The Lord is There." That was the name given to the restored city of God.

This is a great comfort to God's people. God has promised never to leave us or forsake us. Even in the darkest circumstances He is there.

"Yea though I walk through the valley of the shadow of death, I will fear no evil: for thou art with me" Psalm 23:4.

Jacob received that promise from God when he left home. "I am with thee," God said "and will keep thee in all places" Genesis 28:15.

When Moses was called to go and ask Pharaoh to let God's people go, he was very afraid. But God reassured him. "Certainly I will be with thee" Exodus 3:12.

God's promise was sure and He helped Moses in many difficult situations. "My Presence shall go with thee, and I will give thee rest" God promised Moses as they journeyed to the Promised Land.

God promises his presence and companionship to his people, "When thou passest through the waters, I will be with thee" Isaiah 43:2. When we experience difficulties and sadness, it does not mean that God has forgotten us or left us. He is there upholding and strengthening.

When we gather together for worship, God is there. "For where two or three are gathered together in my name, there am I in the midst of them" Matthew 18:20.

Before Jesus ascended to heaven he spoke to his disciples, telling them to make disciples of people in all nations, baptising them and teaching them. His promise was "I am with you alway even to the end of the world" Matthew 28:20.

This is a promise for us today from Jesus, who was called Immanuel- "God with us," and Jehovah Shammah – "the Lord who is there."

 Think Spot: Think about a time when you struggled and felt sad. Did you pray? How does praying to God help you at times like that?

 Thank Spot: Thank God that he is always there and that he doesn't take a break or need a rest. Even when we are asleep he is always awake - he never slumbers.

Bible Search

The initials of the missing words will
spell out a word in the story.

1. "If thy presence go not with me, _____
us not up hence" Exodus 33:15.

2. "When thou passest through the waters,
I will be with thee; and through the rivers,
they shall not _____ thee" Isaiah 43:2.

3. "For where two or three are gathered
together in my name, there am I in the
_____ of them" Matthew 18:20.

4. "But I am _____ and needy, yet the Lord
thinketh upon me" Psalm 40:17.

5. "When thou goest out to battle...be not

_____ of them: for the Lord thy God

is with thee" Deuteronomy 20:1.

6. "He hath said I will _____ leave thee

nor forsake thee" Hebrews 13:5.

7. "Abraham believed God and it was

_____ unto him for righteousness: and

he was called the Friend of God" James 2:23.

8. "Teaching them to _____ all things

whatsoever I have commanded you"

Matthew 28:20.

9. "Let us come before his presence with

thanksgiving, and make a joyful _____

unto him with psalms" Psalm 95:2.

Answer: _____

9. JEHOVAH TSIDKENU

THE LORD OUR RIGHTEOUSNESS

Jeremiah was a prophet who spoke the word of the Lord in the land of Judah. He did this for many years and in very difficult circumstances.

The people of Judah were sinning terribly. Jeremiah continually warned them about their sin and God's judgment. God sent other prophets as well as Jeremiah but nobody would listen to their warnings.

Jeremiah accepted his difficult assignment and spoke out God's word faithfully. You can read what Jeremiah wrote in two Old Testament books: Jeremiah and Lamentations.

Jeremiah feared God and trusted in Him. He had to speak God's word although it was hard and unpopular. He predicted that Judah would be taken captive. Jeremiah knew that the Lord God would deal with the people of Israel because of their sin and disobedience.

But God also sent a message of hope to Israel and Judah. He would raise up a "righteous Branch," a king who would reign and prosper and judge the earth justly. The nation of Israel and Judah would be restored. The Messiah or Saviour would come. His name would be Jehovah Tsidkenu – the Lord our Righteousness.

This promise was fulfilled in the Lord Jesus Christ whose name means Saviour for "he shall save his people from their sins."

David said that the Lord "leadeth me in the paths of righteousness for his name's sake." We can also trust in God to lead us in the right paths.

The name Jehovah Tsidkenu, the Lord our Righteousness, is a glorious name.

We cannot rely on our own works or background or knowledge. There is nothing that you can do or say that can save you from sin. All sin deserves God's anger and punishment.

So do good works mean nothing? The Bible tells us that "All our righteousnesses are as filthy rags" Isaiah 64:6. Our only hope of being right with God is by standing upon His merits, clothed in the robe of Christ's righteousness.

It is only because of God - who he is and what he has done - that we can be brought back to God, and become members of his family.

There was a great Scottish minister, Robert Murray McCheyne. He lived in the city of Dundee. While he was still quite a young man Robert wrote a beautiful poem about Jehovah Tsidkenu. Here is an extract from that poem.

1. I once was a stranger to grace and to God,

   I knew not my danger, and felt not my load;

   Though friends spoke in rapture

   of Christ on the tree,

   Jehovah Tsidkenu was nothing to me.

2. Like tears from the daughters of Zion that roll,

   I wept when the waters went over His soul;

   Yet thought not that my sins had nailed to the
   tree

   Jehovah Tsidkenu 'twas nothing to me.

3. When free grace awoke me,

    by light from on high,

   Then legal fears shook me, I trembled to die;

   No refuge, no safety in self could I see

   Jehovah Tsidkenu my Saviour must be.

4. My terrors all vanished before the sweet name;

   My guilty fears banished, with boldness I came

   To drink at the fountain, life giving and free-

   Jehovah Tsidkenu is all things to me.

Before Robert Murray McCheyne was converted Jehovah Tsidkenu meant nothing to him. Before he came to seek forgiveness for his sins Jesus Christ meant nothing to him. He didn't realise that it was because of his sin that Jesus had died on the cross. But then God showed him that he was a sinner and that he deserved to be punished for sin. Robert was terrified that he would die and face God's judgement, for he knew that because of his sin God's judgement meant eternal death.

Robert had no idea what to do. There was nothing that he could do, he could see that. He needed refuge, he needed to be saved, and the only one who could save him was

God... Jehovah Tsidkenu. Robert knew that Jesus Christ, God's promised Saviour, was the only one who could rescue him from sin and eternal death.

When Robert realised who he had to turn to for Salvation he was no longer terrified. He knew that he could trust in the Lord for his salvation and that he need no longer be afraid of Hell.

Just like a thirsty traveller comes up to a well or a fountain and drinks their fill of cool, clear water, so Robert came boldly up to the Lord and received salvation. The Lord God gave him the gift of eternal life. And as is the case with all gifts - the gift of

Salvation is a free gift - without money and without price.

Further on in the poem Robert talks about how Jehovah Tsidkenu becomes all things to him.

What does Jesus mean to you? Do you love Jesus because he first loved you? Are you sorry for your sin? Do you long to come to the Lord Jesus to have your sins forgiven?

God worked in Robert's life so that the man who cared nothing for Jehovah was changed into one who loved him. In the last verse of the poem Robert says that whatever happens, Jehovah Tsidkenu will always be his song even to death. Jehovah Tsidkenu will bring him joy. He will praise Jehovah's name forever.

This beautiful name for the Lord, Jehovah Tsidkenu, the Lord our Righteousness is our hope too in all the circumstances of life, right to the end.

 Think Spot: Find a dirty dish rag. Look up Isaiah 64:6. Think about how the good things you do are like this dirty rag. Your good words won't get you into heaven.

 Thank Spot: Thank God that the gift of Salvation is free. There is nothing for you to do to gain salvation except believe in the Lord Jesus Christ.

BIBLE SEARCH

The initial letters of the missing words
will spell a word in the story.

1. "Mercy and _____ are met together;
righteousness and peace have kissed each
other" Psalm 85:10.

2. "We do not present our _____
before thee for our righteousnesses, but for
thy great mercies" Daniel 9:18.

3. "Abraham believed God and it was
_____ unto him for righteousness"
James 2:23.

4. "And the heavens shall _____ his
righteousness" Psalm 50:6.

5. "But seek ye first the _____ of God and his righteousness; and all these things shall be added unto you" Matthew 6:33.

6. "Lead me O Lord in thy righteousness because of mine _____: make thy way straight before my face" Psalm 5:8.

7. "He leadeth me in the paths of righteousness for his _____ sake" Psalm 23:3.

8. "If we confess our sins he is faithful and just to forgive us our sins and to cleanse us from all _____" 1 John 1:9.

Answer: _____

10. JEHOVAH MACCADDESHEM

THE LORD WHO SANCTIFIES

God spoke to Moses on Mount Sinai giving him

the Ten Commandments and details of the

law. He gave instructions about the tabernacle,

God's dwelling place and the furnishings and

decorations for it. God reminded Moses of the importance of keeping the Sabbath day holy. "The Sabbath is a sign between Me and you," God said, "so that you will know that I am the LORD who sanctifies you (or makes you holy) - Jehovah Maccaddeshem." This was not meant to be a burden but a wonderful way of remembering all that God had done for them.

The Lord created man and rested on the seventh day, not because he was tired but because he had finished his great work of creation.

The Sabbath was a day to stop from work and remember all that God had done. We remember the Lord's Day in a special way because of what the Lord Jesus Christ did for his people on the cross. He died for them and then rose again three days later. The day of Christ's resurrection is now our Christian Sabbath. Some people call this Sunday, or The Lord's Day. After his resurrection Christ ascended into heaven where he continually prays for us.

The Lord's Day should be a day when we remember him. It is a day of rest and worship.

 Think Spot: Think of the wonderful things that God has done for you today. Now think about what he has done throughout your life.

 Thank Spot: It is good to thank God for what he gives us. Thank him for giving you a special day to rest and think about him.

BIBLE SEARCH

Look up the Bible verses to find the initial letters of the missing words. These will spell out something connected with the story.

1. "Remember the _____ day to keep it holy" Exodus 20:8.

2. "It shall be a Sabbath of rest unto you, and ye shall _____ your souls, by a statute for ever" Leviticus 16:31.

3. "Ye are a chosen generation, a royal priesthood, an holy _____, a peculiar people" 1 Peter 2:9.

4. "God blessed the seventh day, and sanctified it: because that in it he had

rested from all his work which God

_____ and made" Genesis 2:3.

5. "Sanctify them through thy _____"
John 17:17.

6. "Thou art holy, O thou that _____

the praises of Israel" Psalm 22:3.

7. "Holy _____ keep through thine own

name those whom thou hast given me, that

they may be one, as we are" John 17:11.

8. "Submit _____ therefore to God"
James 4:7.

Answer: _____

11. JEHOVAH SABAOTH

LORD OF HOSTS

Isaiah was a prophet who lived in Jerusalem.

God gave him the special duty of speaking his

word to the people of Judah.

God appeared to him in a splendid vision. He

saw the Lord sitting on a throne. Above stood angels. Each angel had six wings – two to cover his face, two to cover his feet and two to fly with. One angel called out to another. "Holy, holy, holy is the LORD of Hosts: the whole earth is full of his glory" Isaiah 6:3.

Jehovah Sabaoth means Lord of Hosts or Lord of great armies. God was the head not only of Israel's armies but of all people and angels. God rules the armies of the whole world.

David knew this. When he faced Goliath the Philistine giant, he could boldly say, "You come with a sword, and a spear and a javelin. But I come to you in the name of the LORD of hosts, the God of the armies of Israel."

David composed a Psalm of praise to the strong and mighty God. "Who is this King of glory?" he asked. "The LORD of Hosts, he is the King of glory" Psalm 24:10.

When we see terrible pictures of wars and fighting in different parts of the world, we must remember that "Our God reigns." He is the LORD of Hosts – Jehovah Sabaoth.

Think Spot: It is amazing to think of our great and powerful God. He is the LORD of Hosts and the King of glory. The Bible tells us that if God is for us no one can be against us. How does that make you feel?

Thank Spot: Thank God that he is totally in charge and that there is nothing that he does not control.

BIBLE SEARCH

The initials of the missing words will spell out

the subject of the story.

1. "Elijah said, As the LORD of hosts

_____ before whom I stand, I will surely

shew myself unto him today" 1 Kings 18:15.

2. "The LORD of hosts is with us; The God

of Jacob is _____ refuge" Psalm 46:7.

3. "But O LORD of hosts that judgest

_____"Jeremiah 11:20.

4. "David...went...to bring up...the ark of

God, whose name is called by the name of

the LORD of hosts that _____ between

the cherubims" 2 Samuel 6:2.

5. "The LORD of hosts is the God _____ Israel," 2 Samuel 7:26.

6. "Holy, holy, holy is the LORD of hosts: The whole earth is _____ of his glory" Isaiah 6:3.

7. "O LORD of hosts, if thou wilt indeed look on the affliction of thine _____ and remember me...I will give him unto the LORD" 1 Samuel 1:11.

8. "For _____ of Jerusalem shall go forth a remnant...The zeal of the LORD of hosts shall do this" Isaiah 37:32.

9. "Except the Lord of Sabaoth had left us a _____ we had been as Sodom and been made like unto Gomorrah" Romans 9.29.

10. "How amiable are thy _____ O

LORD of hosts" Psalm 84:1.

11. "Ye shall know that the LORD of hosts

hath _____ me" Zechariah 2:9.

Answer: _____ ____ _____

ANSWERS

BIBLE SEARCH PAGE 21

Everlasting life; repentance; forgiveness of sins;

salvation; righteousness; faith; love; peace; joy; word;

all things.

BIBLE SEARCH PAGE 28

My; you; banqueting; among; nations; name; ensign;

rejoice.

WORDS: My Banner.

BIBLE SEARCH PAGE 37

Soul; higher; early; poor; heart; eagle's; rod; desires.

WORD: Shepherd

BIBLE SEARCH PAGE 45

Hope; earth; against; leaves; iniquities; need; Gilead.

WORD: Healing

BIBLE SEARCH PAGE 53

Spoken; hearts; author; love; our; minded; preach;

end; abundance; chastisement; earth.

WORDS: Shalom Peace

BIBLE SEARCH PAGE 62

Carry; overflow; midst; poor; afraid; never; imputed;

observe; noise.

WORD: Companion.

BIBLE SEARCH PAGE 75

Truth; supplications; imputed; declare; kingdom; enemies; name's; unrighteousness.

WORD: Tsidkenu

BIBLE SEARCH PAGE 80

Sabbath; afflict; nation; created; truth; inhabitest; Father; yourselves.

WORD: Sanctify.

BIBLE SEARCH PAGE 86

Liveth; our; righteously; dwelleth; over; full; handmaid; out; seed; tabernacles; sent.

WORDS: Lord of Hosts.

OTHER BOOKS

BY CARINE MACKENZIE

The Bible Explorer

ISBN: 978-1-85792-533-3

The Jesus Files

ISBN:978-1-84550-040-5

God, the Ten Commandments and Jesus

ISBN:978-1-85792-850-1

The Names of Jesus

ISBN: 978-1-85792-650-7

IF YOU LIKED THIS

YOU'LL LOVE THESE

God's Book of Wisdom by Belinda Buckland

ISBN: 978-1-85792-963-8

How God Stopped the Pirates by Joel Beeke

ISBN: 978-1-85792-816-7

Children's Devotions by Frances Ridley Havergal

ISBN: 978-1-85792-973-7

The Ten Commandments by Lois Veals

ISBN: 978-1-85792-651-4

CHRISTIAN FOCUS PUBLICATIONS

Christian Focus **Christian Heritage** **CF4K** **Mentor**

Christian Focus Publications publishes books for adults and children under its four main imprints: Christian Focus, CF4K, Mentor and Christian Heritage. Our books reflect that God's word is reliable and Jesus is the way to know him, and live for ever with him.

Our children's publication list includes a Sunday School curriculum that covers pre-school to early teens; puzzle and activity books. We also publish personal and family devotional titles, biographies and inspirational stories that children will love.

If you are looking for quality Bible teaching for children then we have an excellent range of Bible story and age specific theological books.

From pre-school to teenage fiction, we have it covered!

Find us at our web page: www.christianfocus.com

Because you're never too young to know Jesus